WINNING IS
RESPONSIBILITY

WINNING IS RESPONSIBILITY
Copyright © 1988 by
The Winners Series
SRS Enterprises
P.O. Box 1229
Antioch, California 94509

ISBN: 0-938762-27-3

Library of Congress Catalog Card No.: 80-85339

First Edition

First Printing, May 1988

Lithographed in USA by
COMMUNITY PRESS, INC.

WINNING IS
RESPONSIBILITY

Publisher and Editor
Steven R. Shallenberger

Technical Editor
Kathy Grant

Author
Margery Beaudin

Art Illustrator
Jerry T. Christopherson

Advisors

Linda Adams
Michael Call
Paul and Millie Cheesman
Troy and Janet Fullmer
Annette Hullinger
Kirk and Janet Jameson
William and Ellie Jones
Garr and Michelle Judd
Gary and Carla Laney

Tim and Barbara Mitchell
Charles and Kathy Parry
Dan and Esther Randall
Della Mae Rasmussen
Roxanne Shallenberger
Madelyn Starly
Mindy Suttner
Russell and Diane Thoman
Lael and Margaret Woodbury

An SRS Enterprises Publication

Distributed by
Eagle Marketing Corporation

FOREWORD

The Winners Series was developed out of a need and desire by parents, grandparents, teachers, librarians, and church leaders to teach important values and character traits to youth.

Children and youth of all ages enjoy good stories — especially true stories of character and good principles. The stories used in *The Winners Series* have been and will be told over and over, yet they are new and fascinating to every new generation.

These stories need to be retold today so that boys and girls of this century may also see their importance, their beauty, and be inspired by them.

In the publisher's opinion, no greater contribution can be made to our society and toward peace in the world than through teaching youth time-tested principles.

The youth of today will be the leaders of tomorrow. As they identify with inspirational role models and examples, they will be founded in solid values. The values and traits that have made people happy and successful from the beginning of time will be passed from one generation to the next.

In a world where more and more forces challenge us as we seek to do good, we must be more worthy competitors in counter-balancing bad and sordid influences. Where forces work toward the erosion of families and the self-worth of individuals, it is important that people work that much more fervently to strengthen their personal characters and the foundation of good living.

Gratitude and appreciation are expressed to the illustrator, authors, and many individuals who have contributed to the creation and development of *The Winners Series . . . Values for Youth.*

Steven R. Shallenberger, Editor and Publisher

THIS BOOK IS DEDICATED TO BOYS AND GIRLS
IN EVERY CORNER OF THE EARTH WHO SEEK
TO DO GOOD WITH THEIR LIVES.

Other themes in *The Winners Series . . . Values for Youth:*

Winning is . . .

Self-control	Obedience
Moral Cleanliness	Forgiveness
Prayer	Faith
Making, Saving, and Spending Money	Communication
Believing in Yourself	Developing Self
Honesty	Work
Getting Along	A Sense of Humor

6

Hello, welcome to Winners' Town. It's always nice to have visitors. I'm the fire chief here; you can call me Bill. I take good care of Winners' Town—in fact, my job is pretty important. A fire is no joking matter. I always have to be prepared to do my job no matter what. I guess that's why I feel responsibility is so important.

What's that you say? What's so great about responsibility? Well, I know that at first glance it may not seem to take a front seat with all the other important things there are to worry about, but can you imagine what would happen if I didn't do my job in a responsible way? You're right, there probably wouldn't be much of Winners' Town left at all. I remember the last call we got just a few days ago. It was for a small fire in a vacant lot, but it wouldn't have taken long for that little fire to grow into a mighty big one if I hadn't done my job.

Responsibility means that you can see for yourself that there is a job to be done, but it doesn't stop there. It also means that you can get up the gumption to do that job no matter what! It also means that if you say you'll do something, you do it. That's what my job is all about. I told the folks here in Winners' Town that I would be ready to fight any fire, and I am.

But responsibility isn't just important for me, it's important for everyone. You might think that your job isn't as important as a fire chief's, but it is important in its own way. Take homework, for instance; it takes a responsible person to do it and get it turned in. Responsibility also means being dependable and accountable to your employer. I guess it goes along with that important word *loyalty*. And if you think responsibility has something to do with understanding and obeying rules, you're right! Or standing up for another person in a difficult situation. It could mean doing the best job ever the next time you're baby-sitting, or even facing the consequences the next time you make a mistake.

You can see that responsibility has a lot to do with how well we get along with each other and how we feel about ourselves here in Winners' Town. Since you're here, why don't I tell you about what happened when some of the students at the school down the street decided to learn first-hand about responsibility.

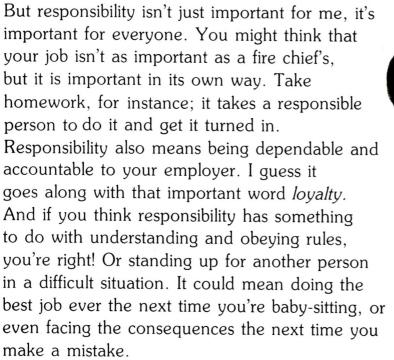

8

It all started one night at a special program the school puts on each year—Parent Appreciation Night. A student named Charlie was first on the program and he walked toward the microphone with a little flutter in his stomach. He stood and looked out over the audience of parents who were all dressed up and looked very interested in what he was going to say. He cleared his throat and began his little speech.

"Tonight is a special night because it gives each of us a chance to tell about our parents. My parents are great! They have always loved me, even before I was born—at least that's what my mom said." When he paused, the parents all smiled and looked at each other. "My dad works hard to give our family a home and all the things we need. But sometimes he takes time out to play ball with us and I really appreciate that. My mom cooks and works for us too and she is always trying to get us to be neat kids, and sometimes we are. I really love her too." With that last comment Charlie blushed and looked like he couldn't remember what he should do next, then he raised his hands in a shrug and said, "Thank you." Charlie returned to his seat on the stage along with the rest of the members of his class. The audience applauded and Charlie's parents smiled proudly.

Next a tall boy with dark hair and large dark eyes came forward. As he stood in front of the microphone, Miss Swenson leaned forward and whispered loudly, "Raise the microphone, Paul." After adjusting the microphone and taking a deep breath, Paul began.

"My mom is very special to me because she really works hard to take care of me and all my brothers and sisters. She works in the morning and then comes home and does all the housework too, and I know that isn't easy." He looked at his mother in the audience. She was smiling at him and her eyes looked large and shiny.

"I also love my dad…" Paul paused for a minute and then said, "I wasn't going to tell this, but I want you all to know what kind of hero my dad really is…

"Last week I went to work with my dad at the train yard where he's a night watchman. When I got tired, he let me take a nap on a cot in the back room at the office. I had been sleeping for a little while when a man's voice woke me up. I started listening and could hear my dad and the man talking together. I guess it was an old friend because they were laughing and joking. Then it got very quiet for a minute and the man told my dad the real reason he had come. He said, 'I've got a plan that could make us both a lot of money. If you leave car #10 unlocked tomorrow night, I'll come and get what I can out of it. No one will ever know you were in on it. Then I'll come back after I sell the loot and split the money with you. What do you say?'

"It was quiet and I wondered what my dad would say to the man. Then I heard my dad answer him.

"He said, 'Listen, that's out of the question. My responsibility is to my employer! He hired me for this job and he pays me to do it the best I can. And that's not where it ends. I have a responsibility to my family. They don't want a thief for a father. And I don't want to have to look at the face of a thief every time I look in the mirror.'

"After my dad said that, it got quiet and I heard the office door close. That man didn't even know how to answer my dad when he said those things, and I was so proud of him I wanted to shout. My dad isn't here tonight because he has to work, and I know he would be embarrassed that I told this whole long story just about him, but I wanted you to know that he is my hero." Paul walked back to his seat. After a moment or two the people began to clap, and they clapped for a long time.

15

It wasn't until the next day at school that Paul realized his speech about his father's responsible actions had made many people stand up and take notice. As the school bell rang that morning, the students quickly took their seats. Miss Swenson put her spelling book on the desk and turned to face the class.

"Well, how did your parents enjoy the program last night?" The students responded with nods and smiles.

"Mine really liked it," Charlie said.

"I enjoyed it too," Miss Swenson answered. "And I've been thinking a lot about what went on there, especially what Paul said about his father." She walked over to the side of the room where Paul was sitting and continued, "Paul's father had an important job to do and he did it. Even though it looked like he could have made a lot of money by helping his friend steal, Paul's dad knew that wasn't a fair or responsible thing to do." The class looked at Paul and he looked shy but proud. "This gave me an idea for our class," she continued. "We could try a secret experiment for the next two weeks—each member of our class would look for ways to act responsibly, like Paul's father or some other great leader we've learned about. When the two weeks are over, we'll talk about the results." The class members just looked at each other with puzzled expressions.

"We can't do what Paul's father did. We don't have jobs," said Tyler.

"That's true, but think about it for a minute," said Miss Swenson. "I wouldn't be surprised if you could find plenty of ways to be responsible here at school or at home. And there are lots of other ways we can be responsible too. Why don't you think it over and maybe you will get some ideas for our secret experiment."

Mark's hand went up and he pointed out, "Miss Swenson, when a scientist does an experiment, he expects something important to happen, like an explosion or something really neat. What could happen with this kind of experiment?"

Miss Swenson smiled and said, "Don't worry. I bet there will be some pretty exciting results, but we'll talk about that in two weeks when we evaluate the experiment."

THINK ABOUT IT:
1. Why was Paul so proud of his father?
2. How did Paul's father show that he was a responsible person?
3. If you were to take part in the secret experiment, what would you choose to do?

Later that afternoon Mark and Tyler walked home together. "What are you going to do for the secret experiment?" Mark asked.

"I don't know yet," said Tyler. "I think Abe Lincoln and Confucius already did all the responsible stuff."

"Well, there must be something left to do," said Mark.

"Keep thinking," said Tyler as he turned up the walk to his house. "And have fun doing your homework," he called to Mark with a laugh.

Mark walked on down the street toward his house. His school books were starting to get heavy and he still had another block to go. It seemed that every day he had to carry these books home—math and history and sometimes spelling and science. Today he had a couple of books for a special history report he was working on. And that's when the idea hit him. He would do his secret experiment on homework!

Mark had been reading a book about Ben Franklin not too long ago and had been amazed at how Ben had been responsible for his own learning. Ben didn't have anyone to give him assignments and to make sure he had the next chapter read by Friday. As a young boy of twelve, Ben Franklin had agreed with his father that the best thing for him would be to learn a trade, but Ben didn't like the way it had to be done. In those days a young boy had to sign an agreement that he would work for his master until he was twenty-one! He was expected to obey his master, keep his master's secrets, and be on duty as his master demanded night and day. This was called apprenticeship, but to Ben it sounded like prison. However, it was the only way to learn a trade, so Ben finally decided to become an apprentice to his older brother James and learn printing.

However, Ben learned the printing business very quickly, and then there he was with nothing to do but work for his brother until he became twenty-one years old. Ben Franklin, being the kind of person he was, decided not to waste the years ahead. Instead, he decided to use his time trying to learn everything he could about every subject.

Ben started out trying to write poetry, but when his father read it he thought it was awful and told Ben he should try something else. So Ben practiced writing letters to his brother's newspaper and signing them with a made-up name so no one would know who had written them. He learned a lot of new words. And the more he practiced, the better he learned to write. He read books about every subject, he observed as much as he could, and he tried to think up new ideas.

Mark's foot hit the front step and he stumbled forward. He had been so deep in thought that he wasn't watching where he was going. He hurried into the house and before his mother even had the chance to say a word, he had his books spread out on the table and he had started his math assignment. His nice sharp pencil lead scratched out the numbers in neat rows and columns, and he was so busy thinking that he didn't see his five-year-old brother standing there watching him. "What are you doing?" Brandon asked.

"Just homework," Mark answered.

"Well, don't you need a TV to do that?" asked Brandon.

"Not really," Mark smiled, "in fact, it works much better without one."

"But you usually do your homework by the TV," Brandon insisted.

"Not today, Brandon—today I am being responsible for my own learning instead of just getting the work done," Mark replied.

Brandon wandered off to play and Mark sat tapping his pencil against his front tooth. This must have been what Mr. Ortega had been talking about. It had been a long time since he had thought about Mr. Ortega, his fourth grade teacher. At the beginning of that year, Mr. Ortega had come into the classroom with a tray, two cups, and a large pitcher of water.

"Class, I want to give you a little demonstration on learning. These cups represent each one of you students. See how they stand here happily, ready to learn. And here I am, the teacher," he said, indicating the pitcher. "Yes, I am like this pitcher, full of wonderful things to teach you. And I'm going to do my best to do that job. I will pour knowledge into each of you." And then Mr. Ortega had started to pour the water from the pitcher into the cups. But suddenly the water had started to splash and spill and Mark had leaned over his desk to see what was happening. One of the cups had been turned upside-down and the water was running off. Mr. Ortega had looked at the class and smiled, "Please, be ready to receive the wonderful things I have to teach you this year, and don't turn your cup over!"

At the time Mark had thought it was a pretty neat demonstration, but it wasn't until now that he felt he really knew what it meant to have his cup ready to receive. He was excited as he finished the math assignment. He had really learned the idea rather than just doing the work. He looked at the page for the next day and read it over carefully. Yes, he understood some of it, but he would have a few questions for his teacher the next day.

Next he opened his history book and dived in. It was amazing how different things were when he was learning because he wanted to. The table was covered with charts, lists, maps, and diagrams he had made to help him learn and remember the information from the chapter. He was concentrating intently on the Industrial Revolution when he looked up to see his mother's concerned face.

"Are you feeling all right?" she asked.

"Sure, Mom."

"You don't have a fever, do you?"

"No, Mom," Mark answered.

"Well, it's almost time for me to fix dinner so I'll need you to clear up your school things," she said. Mark started gathering up his papers and arranging them in order so they would be easy to refer to in class tomorrow.

"You must have something new to study today," Mark's mother said, still looking a bit surprised.

"Oh, no," said Mark, "just more of the same."

"Well, it's really great to see you studying so hard. You must be growing up," she said as she began chopping an onion on the wooden cutting board.

"I must be," said Mark as he stacked his books one on top of another. This sure was an improvement, he thought to himself. When it came to homework it had seemed there was always a bone to be picked between him and his mother, but today things were different. He kind of liked it better this way.

THINK ABOUT IT:
1. How did Mark show that he was responsible?
2. How do you feel when you go to school unprepared? Prepared?
3. What did Mr. Ortega's demonstration mean?
4. What are some things you would like to do to be more responsible for your own learning?

27

After walking home with Mark that afternoon, Tyler had started thinking seriously about the secret experiment. Something responsible, like a great citizen—that was what Miss Swenson had said. That evening he sat by his dad while he watched the six o'clock news. The commentator talked about a lot of different people—some government leaders, some criminals, some people who had climbed a mountain. Tyler's mind started to wander.

"And now a news flash..." said the commentator. "I have just received a wire story stating that Tyler Johnson of Winners' Town has performed a responsible deed!"

"Well, maybe my imagination is out of hand," Tyler thought to himself. He listened to the news for a little while longer and then got up and wandered into his bedroom and lay back on his bed. It would be nice to do something so great that it could be on the news, but then most of the stories on the news were about people who did things that were anything but responsible.

Before he knew it, several days had passed and it was Sunday. Tyler, dressed in his Sunday best clothes, sat in his Sunday School class watching his teacher place a flannel board on the table. She had several cutout pictures with sandpaper squares pasted on the back and was starting to tell a story.

As Tyler listened, he realized he had heard the story many times before, but this time as his teacher spoke, it was as if Tyler were actually there, watching the story take place. He could almost see the man dressed in biblical style robes walking along the dusty road in sandaled feet. The man seemed to be in a hurry and he kept glancing back every few steps. At the sound of footsteps from behind the rocks at the side of the road, the man began to run—but it was no use. The robbers came out from their hiding place and the biggest man with shaggy hair grabbed the fleeing traveler. The other two robbers ran forward and the three of them raised their fists and started beating the traveler. He held up his arms to defend himself, but it was no use. The three men knocked him to the ground and pulled his coat from him. "Get the money pouch," commanded the large one. When they had all of his belongings, the three disappeared up into the rocky hills from which they had come.

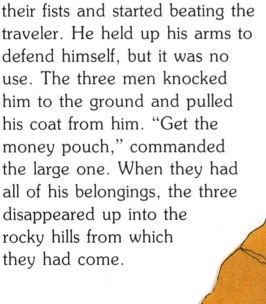

The traveler tried to rise on one hand, but then fell forward and lay still. The late afternoon was deepening into evening and the shadows were growing long. After a while another figure came along the dusty road to Jericho. One could tell by his clothing that he was a priest. As he approached the wounded traveler, he seemed to look carefully and closely at the figure on the road, but then he looked around and began to walk faster on the other side. The fallen man moaned softly, but the priest hurried on.

Time passed and a Levite approached. The man moaned again, but the Levite reacted the same way the priest had; he hurried on without stopping to help. The traveler must have thought that there was no help for him at all, and he tried unsuccessfully to rise again, but he could not.

It was then that the Samaritan came along the road with his little donkey, and seeing the man lying there, he walked closer. The Samaritan knelt beside the man and when he saw how badly he was wounded, he hurried over to his little donkey to bring back leather pouches of oil and wine. He carefully poured their contents into the traveler's wounds, then gently bandaged the man and lifted him up onto the back of the donkey.

By now the purple dusk had become night. The Samaritan brought the wounded traveler to an inn. There he saw to it that the man was cared for properly and given all that he needed. As he left, the Samaritan offered the host money to pay for further care and told him he would pay for anything else that was needed on his return.

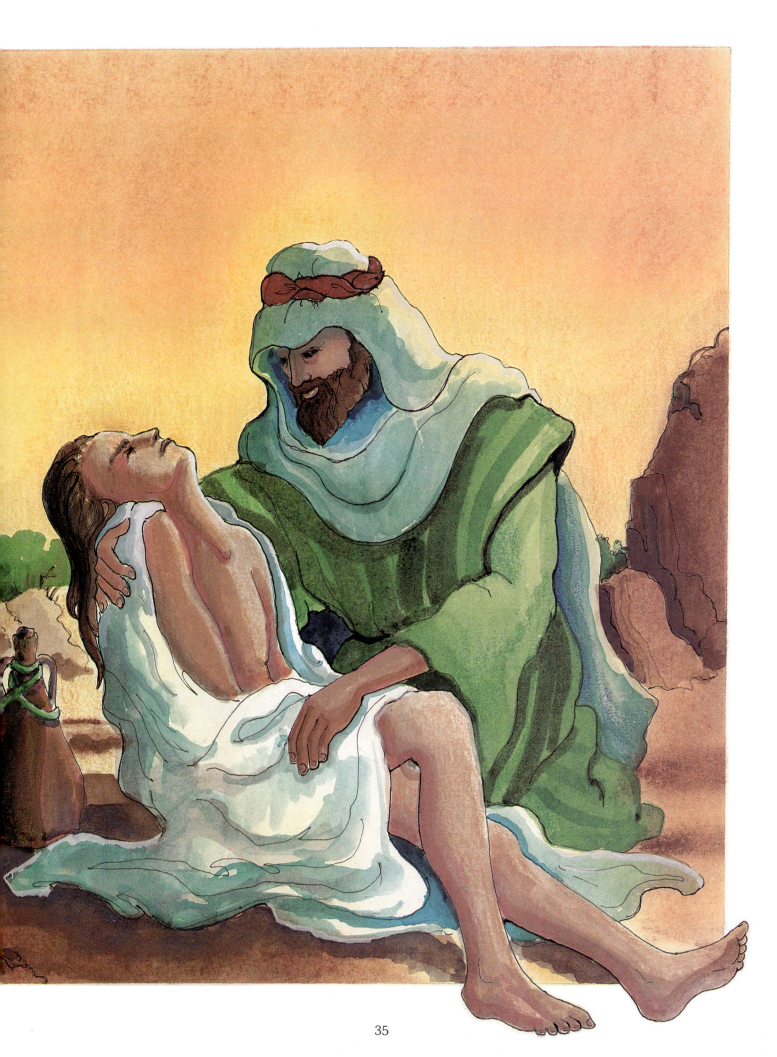

"And now, Tyler, what do you think of the Good Samaritan?" asked the Sunday School teacher with a smile as she took her flannel board figures down.

"Well," said Tyler, his imaginings interrupted, "I think he was very, ah...responsible," and then he smiled. This secret experiment was making him look at everything quite differently than he used to.

"That's an interesting comment," said his teacher. "What makes you say that?"

"The Good Samaritan saw a job to do and he did it, even though the robbers could have come back and beat him up too," said Tyler. "I guess we should be responsible for others, and stand up for them and help them."

"That's right, Tyler," his teacher responded, smiling. "Thank you."

That's it, said Tyler to himself as he sat there watching his teacher, but not hearing a word she was saying. I want to do something really great like helping someone who is almost dead, or at least hurt really badly. Maybe I'll get on the news or be written about in a really famous book— well, probably not as famous as the Bible, but some book. But no situations of that kind came along.

It was a couple of days later that Tyler went over to Glen's house after school. Glen was planning a party and he asked Tyler to help him decide on the people to invite and think up some really fun things to do. Christina came over too. Tyler was pretty excited. He always admired Glen and Christina and was happy to be included in their circle of friends. They were the ones who were always having parties and they were popular, too.

"What do you think of the list so far?" asked Glen, as the three of them sat together in the family room. Glen held up the list and read off the names he had already written. "Kim, Jenny, Blake, Paul, Mark...now we need a couple of girls and another boy."

"How about Ashley or Jessica?" said Christina, as she reached over and took another chip from the bowl that Glen's mother had brought in for the three of them.

"Or how about Kathleen and Benjie?" Tyler volunteered.

"Sure, they'd be fun," said Glen.

"Or we could invite Caroline—she's really nice," said Tyler.

"Caroline!" Glen and Christina exclaimed. "You've got to be kidding! She would be a drag at the party with that big brace thing on her leg. She couldn't dance or anything," said Glen.

"Well, she is nice," responded Tyler.

"No one would want to be with her. She's too different," said Christina.

"Lots of people would like to be with her. I don't understand why you feel that way. What if everyone felt that way? She would never get to go to parties or anything. She's a nice person and she has feelings too. I don't think it's fair," Tyler said. "I think we should invite her."

"Whose party is this, anyway?" said Glen. "I have final say on who's coming and I say she's not."

Suddenly Tyler was very disappointed. He had been so happy to think that Glen wanted him as a friend, and now they were having this disagreement. For a moment he looked at Glen and Christina sitting there, then he said, "Okay, you're right. It is your party." Tyler picked up his school books and jacket and started to walk toward the door. He just couldn't understand them acting like that.

Christina gave Glen a look and snickered, but Glen turned toward Tyler. "Come on, Tyler, Caroline isn't worth it. Let's finish planning the party."

"Well, personally I think she *is* worth it. It doesn't matter if she has a leg brace! I don't think we should act that way towards her," Tyler responded, as he glanced at Christina.

"Oh, come on, Glen, let him go. He doesn't know who the really fun people are," Christina said.

Tyler looked at the two of them standing there looking at him. "Glen, I guess you can cross my name off your list. I don't think I'd have much fun at that kind of party."

But by the time Tyler reached the corner he was feeling angry at himself. Why had he acted that way? Now Glen would never want to be his friend again. But he couldn't deny that Caroline was a nice person and it wasn't right to talk about her like that. He just had to stand up for her; it was his responsibility.

That was when it hit him. He was standing up for another person. That had been his responsibility! Tyler was excited and he found himself walking quickly. He realized that taking the responsibility had been hard, but now he felt great, and that was the result. When you do what you should, you feel great!

THINK ABOUT IT:
1. In what way can you be like the Good Samaritan?
2. Have you ever defended a friend?
3. What would you have said to Glen and Christina if you were in Tyler's place?

Kim checked the spine of the big red book for the letter "N" and then pulled it off the shelf. She had decided to find out more about Florence Nightingale for the secret experiment that her class was doing. Someone as famous as Florence Nightingale must have been responsible in some way, and besides, Kim had always been kind of interested in nursing. She sat reading at the big dark wood table in the library and imagined what Florence Nightingale was like.

Florence had been born in a wealthy family. Her mother liked to have lots of guests and parties,

but Florence preferred studying her Greek, Latin, and mathematics books over joining the parties. One of her favorite things to do was to care for the babies of the people who visited her mother and father. She also loved to pretend that her dolls were sick and nurse them back to health. Once when an old shepherd's dog broke its leg she begged to have a chance to care for it so that the dog would not have to be put to sleep. Her expert care made it possible for the dog's leg to heal properly. She had saved its life.

At the age of sixteen Florence Nightingale decided that she would dedicate her life to the service of others, but it wasn't until later in her life that she was able to go into nursing and do many of the things that made her famous.

As Kim read on, she learned that Florence's mother did not agree with her about her desire to help the poor and suffering, and finally Florence had to leave her family. She went to a hospital in Paris to study nursing. Later she took a small group of nurses to care for wounded soldiers during a war. She did such a good job that everyone praised her and asked for her advice.

Kim thought about what she had read as she jotted down some notes in her notebook. Florence Nightingale had certainly seen that there was an important job to be done. Even though she didn't have much help, she had done a very good job of caring for the wounded soldiers. An idea was already forming in Kim's mind as she closed her notebook and replaced the encyclopedia on the shelf. It was the way Florence did her job that was so important. She was organized and she made sure that the soldiers got the things they needed. Kim had a chance to do something like that right away. She had a baby-sitting job tomorrow night. She wouldn't be caring for wounded soldiers, but she would be caring for children, and they were important.

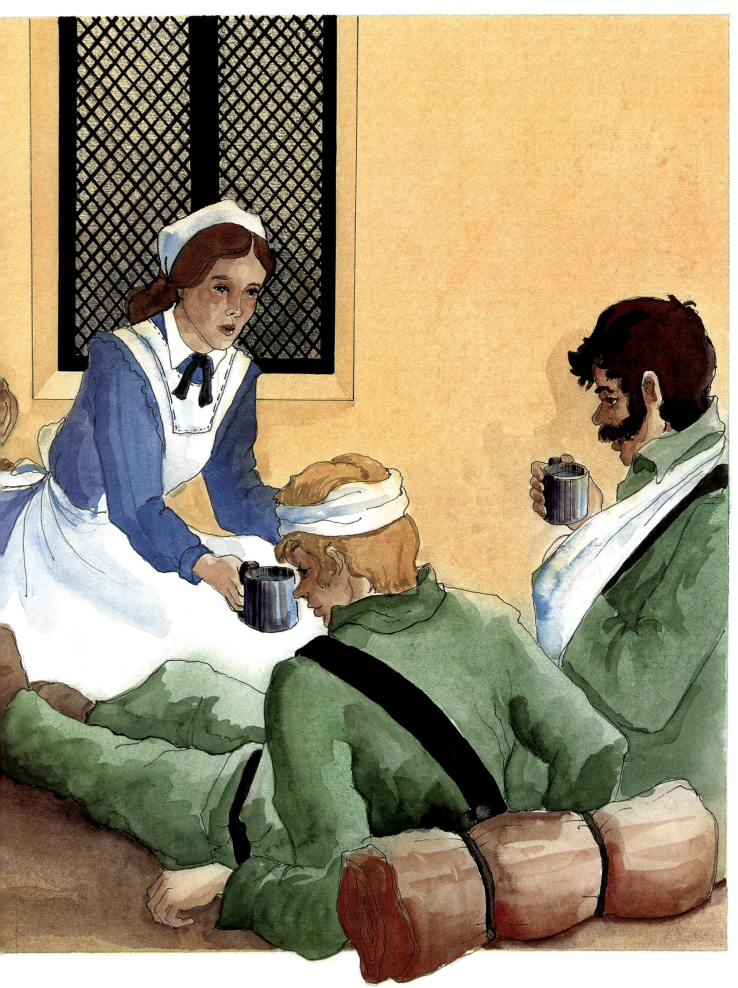

As she walked home from the library she made a list in her mind of the things she would need to do her job well. How about some story books and games? She would bring some from home that would be new to the children. Maybe she should study up on first aid. Maybe she could bring some kind of snack...

When she walked up the steps of the Taylor's house the following evening she carried her gym bag with her. Mrs. Taylor opened the door and welcomed her. "Hello, Kim, what's in the bag?" she asked.

"Oh, just a few things to help me do my job," answered Kim.

Kim looked around the room and could see that Mrs. Taylor had been in a hurry to get ready to go. The children's toys were still scattered around and from where she stood she could see into the kitchen where the dishes were stacked on the counter waiting to be washed. "Where are Alex and Jenny?" she asked.

"Oh, they're downstairs watching television. You can put them to bed at 7:30 and we should be home around 9:30."

Mrs. Taylor got her coat out of the closet and called to her husband, "Hurry, Jerry, or we'll be late."

Mr. Taylor came hurrying into the room still fixing his tie. He pulled on his coat, the two of them said good-bye, and they hurried out the door.

Kim went right to work. First she unzipped her gym bag and pulled out paper and a pencil which she placed beside the phone. She looked around the kitchen and living room again. Yes, there certainly was a job to be done. But first things first. As she hurried down the stairs, she could hear the loud noise of the TV. There she found the children mesmerized by the color and movement on the screen.

"Hi, Jenny and Alex, what are you doing?" she called out happily to the children.

"Hi, Kim," they exclaimed. "You came!"

Kim had been baby-sitting Alex and Jenny ever since their family had moved in next door to her two years ago. The children already loved her, but tonight she would be the best baby-sitter she could be. She didn't bring her homework, and she didn't plan on watching TV all evening. The children had an hour before their bedtime and she was going to make the most of it with them.

"I have a great idea," she said. "Let's go upstairs and look at some of the things I brought in my bag."

"All right, let's!" said Alex.

Kim took the children by the hand and together they started up the stairs.

"Uh oh," said Jenny, "I'll turn off the television." She ran back and pushed the off button and then ran up the steps to join Kim and Alex.

The time flew by, and before Kim knew it, it was time to get the children ready for bed.

"Kim, that story you read about the wild things was really neat," said Alex as he pushed his arms through the sleeves of his pajamas.

"And I liked the game with those red and blue things you flip into the cup," said Jenny. She was already dressed in her nightgown and was going with Kim to brush her teeth.

"We did have a lot of fun," said Kim. "Let's see how quickly we can get our teeth brushed and pick up all the toys in the living room."

"Oh, Kim, let's not pick up the toys. There are too many," said Alex.

"Anyone who helps me gets a piggyback ride to their bed and one more story afterward," said Kim.

The teeth were brushed and the toys were picked up in no time and the children each had a ride on Kim's back as she took them into their bedrooms. After reading them another story, she tucked them into bed. She made sure Jenny's night light was on and got Alex his drink of water. Then she went to the kitchen. "Hmmm," she said, "no phone messages yet."

She hurried around the kitchen straightening things up and then she rinsed the dishes and placed them in the dishwasher. Things were going pretty well, she thought. The children had certainly enjoyed the books and games from her bag. She would have to bring them again next time. And now the living room and kitchen looked neat and clean. Just then the telephone rang and Kim ran over and picked up the receiver. With her other hand she had the pencil ready. "Hello, Taylor's residence," she said.

"Hello, Kim, this is Mrs. Taylor. How are things going?" said the voice on the telephone.

"Just fine, Mrs. Taylor. The children went to bed like angels and they are both asleep now."

"That's great! I just wanted to check. Thanks, Kim. We should be home in a little while," said Mrs. Taylor.

"Okay, see you then," answered Kim. She hung up the phone and looked disappointedly at the paper and pencil. Then she picked up the pencil and carefully wrote: 9:00 p.m. Mrs. Taylor called.

THINK ABOUT IT:
1. Why is it so important for a nurse to be responsible?
2. What other professions need extremely responsible people? Why?
3. Think of five things you could do to show responsibility while baby-sitting.

Kent walked across the grass in front of the school and brushed the hair out of his face with his hand. "What a dumb idea," he thought to himself. "This secret experiment is a waste of time. Who would go out and do something responsible if they didn't have to? Not me! Besides, I can't think of anyone famous to be like." Kent crossed the street and walked past the little grocery store with green crepe paper decorating the dirty windows. "Besides," he thought to himself, "the people I know don't go around doing responsible things all the time. Well, I guess I do know Paul's father and he really did something great. That was pretty amazing how he could turn down all that money just because it came from selling stolen things, and he wouldn't even help the man steal by leaving the boxcar unlocked."

Kent shoved his hands into his jacket pockets and suddenly a shock of guilt went through his whole body. In his pocket his hand had touched a small calculator that wasn't his. It had been there since Monday when he had slipped it off the teacher's desk while she was out in the hall talking to another teacher. At the time he had thought it was such a smart thing to do. He had needed one like that for his math class and he couldn't afford to buy one. Later when Miss Swenson had asked if anyone had seen it he just sat there as she looked around at the class. No one had said anything, and she had just shrugged her shoulders and said that maybe she had taken it home.

Kent spotted a garbage dumpster in the alley by the grocery store and he thought quickly that it would be a good

56

idea to get rid of the calculator and then no one would know and he wouldn't get caught. Besides, he didn't like that guilty feeling that came over him every time he thought about what he had done. So he took the calculator out of his pocket and climbed onto the dumpster.

But then he stopped—what had Miss Swenson ever done to him to make him treat her in such a mean way? If the truth were known, he really did like her. Of course it wouldn't help her much if he threw the calculator away. He should probably slip it back on her desk the same way he had taken it. That was a good idea. He put the calculator back in his pocket and started back towards the school.

As he got closer he saw that Miss Swenson's car was still in the parking lot and he wondered if he could get into the classroom while she was down at the office or somewhere. He walked slowly down the dim hallway and looked from a distance through the open door of her room, Room 24.

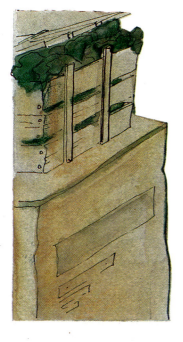

He couldn't see her and he approached slowly, still searching the room with his eyes. This was his chance—he moved quietly on the soft soles of his tennis shoes across the room towards her desk and took the calculator out of his pocket.

It was then that he heard the closet door bang back and he turned to see Miss Swenson with her arms filled with books, pushing back the closet door with her foot. Kent quickly shoved the calculator back in his pocket, hoping she hadn't noticed. Miss Swenson came forward and placed the books on her desk. "Oh, hi there, Kent, did you forget something?" she asked.

Kent wasn't quite sure what to say at first, then a story popped into his head. "Oh, yes, I forgot my English book, and I remembered as I was walking home that we had an assignment."

"That's really great that you remembered your homework," she said. "It's lucky I was still here."

"Yes, I..." Kent felt his fingers touching the calculator again and he just stood there for a moment. He could see that there was a better way to handle the situation than just waiting until she was gone to put back the calculator. But he didn't want to do it. He didn't want to tell her he was the one who had taken it. He stood there just looking down.

"Is something the matter?" she asked.

"I...yes," he said, "something is the matter. I am the one who took your calculator and I wanted to give it back. I was just going to put it on your desk, but I guess it's better to tell you." He held the calculator out toward Miss Swenson waiting for her reaction. She stood still for a moment and then walked over and took it from his hand.

"Thank you, Kent," she said. "That took a lot of courage for you to face up to me and admit what you did."

"I hadn't meant to, but I guess this is the best way to handle it," Kent said. "What are you going to do?"

"Mainly, I am happy to have it back, and also I am proud of you for returning it and taking responsibility for your own actions. It was a mistake and it doesn't have to happen again." She smiled at him and then she said, "This can be our secret."

"Thanks," said Kent. "I guess I did try out the secret experiment after all, even though I didn't mean to."

As he turned and started to leave the classroom, he halfway shrugged and smiled sheepishly, "You must be a good teacher, Miss Swenson. Nobody ever got me to do that before!"

THINK ABOUT IT:
1. What kind of change did Kent make in his life?
2. What was so difficult about what Kent did?
3. Have you ever taken responsibility for a mistake? How did you feel?

The two weeks passed and the day for the discussion of the class's experiment arrived. The students sat down in their seats at the sound of the bell and looked at Miss Swenson expectantly. She looked up from her roll book and then walked around her desk.

"We will start off our homeroom class today by going ahead with our discussion of the secret experiment. I hope all of you had an opportunity to try it. From what I have seen personally, there have been some terrific results—just about as great as an explosion, Mark!" she said with a little laugh. "Would any of you like to tell us about your experiences these last two weeks in connection with the experiment?"

Several hands went up and comments were made about how surprised many parents had been when the dishes were done, the beds were made and the garbage was taken out without their having to remind anyone about it. Charlie told how he had taken special care to put the newspapers right on the front porch in front of the door of every house on his paper route. He was being a responsible paper boy.

Kim raised her hand and said, "I just wanted to say that responsibility made me a lot of money!" She smiled and then added, "After my baby-sitting job at the Taylor's last week, Mrs. Taylor was so pleased with the responsible job I did that she told two of her friends, and they called me to baby-sit for them on the weekend! It was great, and I'm getting calls from their friends now too."

"We have a lot of positive feedback," said Miss Swenson, "but did anyone have a hard time being responsible?"

"Well, I did in a way," volunteered Tyler, "but after everything was over, I felt good because I had done the right thing even though it was hard and I felt kind of unhappy at first."

"That's the way it works sometimes, isn't it," Miss Swenson said. "Does anyone have any last comments?" she asked, walking back to her desk.

"I learned that sometimes it isn't easy to be responsible, but I sure felt like a lot better person after I tried it," said Kent.

"Thanks, Kent," she said as she gave him a special smile. "That's a good note to end on."

She leaned back on the edge of her desk and said, "I hope this won't be the end of it, though. Responsible behavior is a great habit to get into."

Well, what do you think of the young people we have around here? I can tell you we're mighty proud of them. They each met responsibility head-on and each one of them learned something important. They learned how to see a job and do it even when it was hard. The interesting thing is that they didn't all start out as winners, but that's sure the way they ended up.

You know, there is always room for one more in the secret experiment—why don't you join them? Try to do something responsible. It doesn't have to be a great big thing, like fighting fires; in fact, that's a job for someone like me, a fire chief. But you could just start small like they did. Find out what kind of difference it can make in your life. I know you'll be a winner too!

Come back again soon. We always love visitors here in Winners' Town. See you next time!